Keep Me Sane

Keep Me Sane

Sarah Cowan

KEEP ME SANE

Published by Sarah Cowan, Edmonton, Canada

ISBN:
Paperback   978-1-77354-451-9
     ebook   978-1-77354-470-0

Publication assistance and digital printing in Canada by

PAGEMASTER
PUBLISHING
PageMaster.ca

Contents

The Sorrows

House Fire

I am a house fire.
A fire that cannot be controlled.
Destroying every little thing in its track,
burning till there is nothing but ash.

I am a house fire.
With a mind that cannot be controlled.
Destroying every person in my path,
suffocating myself and those around me,
till there is nothing left but me.
Alone in my own disaster.

Alone

Mentally,
Emotionally,
Physically,
Spiritually.
Alone.

Shreds

Forever has come to an end.
I thought you were forever.
My forever.
But you'd rather carve out my heart,
tearing it into a million tiny pieces.
Rather than helping me piece it all back together.

Beautiful Disaster

Healing is suffocating but enlightening.
It's sobbing at 3:00am about your past,
then waking up and managing to forgive
yourself for being broken.
It's the restlessness and panic
of failing yourself,
in fear of not flourishing.
Then later feeling whole,
even if it's only for a brief moment.

Healing is not linear.
It is a series of harsh jagged lines,
of highs and lows all bringing you healing.
Even if it does not feel like it.
But you will rejuvenate.
Over time, you will revive that happy soul of yours.

Because healing is enlightening but suffocating.

Afraid of Endings

I am afraid of endings.
Ours, in particular.
I cry out for it to haunt someone else
but it pollutes only my mind,
fogging my clarity.

If we do reach that dreaded finish line,
there will be nothing left.
But I refuse to reach the end of us.
Because I know I'll despise it.

So I hide,
distract myself,
overwork myself
to avoid confronting
this feeling
of impending doom.

Here

I am here.
Existing, but not living.

Fly Away

Take me away from here.
Physically and mentally.
Put me on a plane, ticket going anywhere.
Anywhere but here:
my own thoughts.
Take me to a new home where peace and tranquility
roams the air that will
fill my lungs,
where negative energies get left at the door.
Help me get unchained from all my thoughts,
all my responsibilities.
Put me on a plane to anywhere but here.

In The Dark

I lay here thinking of You.

Pain throbs in my chest,
reliving old memories like a film.
Stuck in the past,
I find myself in an endless loop.
Fearing the comforting yet familiar
darkness of You.

June 18, 2018

We said our final goodbye today.
Despite our past of loving one another,
we went out for coffee one last time.
Simply to attempt to clear the air before we leave one another for good.
You and I sat at the same table that I once fell in love with you at.
That time was on our first date.
But as we sit across from each other months later,
the emotions are different.

Afterwards, I thanked you for coming out with me, despite my soul aching.
I asked for a quick hug, but we stood in each other's embrace for a long
    moment.
Much longer than I anticipated. But I didn't move away until you did.
Attempting to absorb this moment as I know that will be my last time
I get to hold you in my arms.
"As much as I don't want this to be a goodbye, I just want to thank you
    for everything"
I said to You.
You replied with, "You as well".
I painfully turned my back towards you, leaving you and all we had
    behind.

   -    I guess we were never meant to be.

People I Have Known

She must be off living with her boyfriend,
attending university and building herself a stable career.
Living her best, quiet life.

I'm sure he is enjoying his time with his girlfriend,
the one he cheated on me with,
likely continuing a life with her that I once imagined us having.

She has to be enjoying living in a new atmosphere,
but growing every day as life continuously tests her daily
with all kinds of unimaginable things.

He must be attending university to build his dream career.
Alone with likely no friends,
just like how he was in high school.

- But I do know they're all living their best lives without me.

Numb

I sluggishly crawled out of bed,
feeling off today.
Not happy, nor sad.
I woke up feeling numb,
wishing I could sleep forever.

Cinderella

My dear, Cinderella,
Please dry your tears.

That one man had changed you.
Giving you caution
on finding your true prince.

Grim Reaper

Gripping your hand tightly,
salty tears streaming down my face.
The Grim Reaper knocks on our door,
greeting you with a smile.
"You're not welcome." I say,
"Not yet".
I plead, begging for just a bit more time.

"It is time," He says to me.
And just like that,
you were stolen from me.
Taking my heart with you.

Nothing

Allowing myself to plunge in my thoughts,
I am greeted by an empty box.
Filled with nothing but a heavy void.
This hollow box and my mind interlock,
bringing me silence and nothingness.

Isolated

Alone in my home.
Can't leave.
Sick of the world.
Not allowed to leave.
Sick of my never ending misery.
Isolated from society.
Off in my own bubble.

Beautifully Broken

I have been broken,
I have been stomped on,
I have been betrayed.

But yet

I have been called beautiful,
I have been lifted from those around me,
I have been loved by many.

But yet here I am
feeling beautifully broken.

Overthink

You never leave my mind.
There is never a point in time where
I am thinking of somebody else.
You occupy my mind more than
a hummingbird hovers around
their favorite Bee Balm flower.
I constantly wonder what you are doing,
hoping that you are thinking of me too
despite your busy days.
I live my days and nights worrying.
Overthinking about
whether I am good enough.
Whether you are even thinking of me too.
Overanalyzing every moment,
every breath,
every conversation.
I play out every horrid scenario in my mind
but yet I choose to stay here.
Choosing you every day of my life
and still choosing you for many years to come.
I pray that I don't screw this one up
because I can't lose you too.

Melancholy

Depression weighs me down like an anchor at sea.
I drown
trying to breathe underwater.
I let out a muffled scream,
begging for a hand.
For someone to save me.
For someone to pull me out.
I sink deeper into the ocean,
now reaching the point of no return.

I stop everything.

I stop struggling.
I stop reaching out for help.
I simply allow the water to burn my lungs
as I drown in everything that surrounds me.

How can I float when everything weighs me down?

Stuck

I know you are my person.
But my heart aches
thinking that maybe you will find
someone better.

I don't want to love someone else;
I want you.

My mind demands me to stay.
To battle for what is mine.
But I can't help but wonder
why am I always crying and
feeling so stuck.

On My Bedroom Floor

It is at the dead of night.
We're on the phone.
You're talking to me
and my sole focus is to contain my tears.
Suppressing a panic attack before it begins.
Rage boils over within me,
I try to scream but nothing comes out.
Unable to process any and all emotions or thoughts.
Urges arise from me to let myself feel pain again.
Changing all my mental pain all into physical pain.
I withhold myself from doing so
because I have been clean for so long.
All because of You
encouraging me not to.
I have been doing so well, so far.

My panicked rage results in my phone flying across the room.
You're still on the other end.
The silence becomes deafening to my ears.
Sent to my knees, I weakly collapse.
Collapse into a blubbering mess
on my bedroom floor.

Kill Me Softly

I want to disappear:
mentally and physically.
In every way
take me away.
My life is miserable,
just like me.

Kill me,
as I would be okay
away from my pain.

Morph

Reading old memories,
noticing how I always shift for others.
Building myself to their standards,
tearing down my true self.

Would you like me better if I was how you wanted?
If I did everything you asked?
Would you love me more?
Or love me less?

- I did everything you asked

Multiverse

If the multiverse does exist,
I wish that my life was a bit different.
Good parents.
The kind who both supported me since birth,
even at every sporting event.
The kind who strived to be there for me
at all stages of my life.
I hope that my life was better
with no trauma.
Where I didn't have to have unhealed childhood trauma
that continues to haunt me in my adult years.
I hope that my life was different.
Where I didn't live in a constant state of anxiety.
Where depression does not weigh me down,
ruining an infinite amount of life changing possibilities.

May we meet in another lifetime,
where everything is different.

The Fall of Atlas

The kind of person to carry everyone else's burdens.
To ensure that everyone else's priorities are taken care of,
leaving our own problems behind.

Not only do I have my world on my shoulders,
I willingly choose to carry everyone else's.
And they all just accept it,
not offering a hand to help.

But when I fall,
no one will be there for me.
I will just be questioned why I failed.

Where Fire Meets Fire

Anger builds within us.
There is nothing but tension.
I crave to get away from you,
but you keep pulling me closer.

Please let me leave
because this fire is only getting bigger.

Return

```
The lover,
not possessing any love or lust,
kisses the hopeless slave.

-  Yet the slave returns to you, and loves you again.
```

Mo(u)rning

Brilliant morning shewed that night was dead.
The always slow risen sun
brightens our sky,
giving us a new start to our day.

The sky drifts with blue and white,
gracefully blowing past.

But today is day one without you.
My true sunlight is gone.
My mourning is dark.
Nothing like the sky above me.

Knight

The princess beamed as she watched the Knight
disappear into the sunset.
Continuing to stare long after he waved goodbye,
she broke and threw herself to the ground
crying once he was out of sight and gone for good.

Dirty Sheets

Laying on my bed of sorrow,
I feel filthy.

Not because of enduring something fun
like gardening in the summer sun.
But by knowing that your hands caressed hers
when we were together.
How your lips kissed hers
as I still loved every piece of you.
How you wooed her over behind my back
while you lied to me.
Pretending that everything was okay.

You make me feel dirty,
 unlovable,

not good enough.

I didn't even commit the crime,
but I feel like the blood is on my hands.

- How could you do this to me?

Strong One

No one checks in on the strong one
because people assume that they are doing just fine.
In reality, that is not always the case.
People don't know that I am one step closer to falling off the deep end.

-   Someone please just check in on the strong ones

Bleeding Ears

I cover my adolescent ears with my palms,
attempting to muffle the screams of my parents in the other room.
This foreign feeling of being scared and anxious runs through me,
wishing I could disappear or stop them from fighting.
But I am too scared to step foot into the next room.

I jump at the sound of glass smashing on the hardwood floor.
Pressing my palms into my ears harder than before.

Please make this stop.
Please make this stop.
Please make this stop.
I repeat to myself
over and over again.

Built for Sin

This world is built off of lies and deceit.
From the start, Adam and Eve sinned.
Humanity cannot be perfect humans.
We are all flawed;
We are all built for sin.

-   You're not as innocent as you may seem

He Chose Her

I never should have held your hand or kissed your lips
because I would've saved myself from
my hopes rising higher than the sky above us.
It would have freed me from an aching heart,
longing for someone who didn't even choose me.

Lurk

I feel your presence on my social media.
Not a photo or video has been liked by You,
but I know you're there.
Lurking in the shadows.

Some things I may not ever know:
your thoughts
or what you think of me now.
But that doesn't mean I think
I can still read you like a book.

- I feel your presence, even if you don't think I can

Routine

My alarm goes off at 9:00am.
I put on the same dirty work uniform
that I wore yesterday.
Day in, and day out.
I get myself ready for another long day at work,
surviving that typical full time job.
Then once the day is done,
I arrive back in my home
with no one to greet me at the door.
I do barely passable self care
before I fall asleep in my cold bed.
Before I wake up alone.

To start the same routine all over again.

Drive By

Driving past my old childhood home,
now inhabited by unfamiliar faces.
I notice the comfort in returning to a place that was once mine.

Without my own acknowledgement,
there was later a time when I drove past my old home
for the last time, without even knowing it was the last time.

Driving past my old childhood home
is not the same as it once was.
But that doesn't mean this isn't the same place where memories roam.

Piece Me Back Together

My love, if you want to heal,
learn to not change the past
or worry about the future.
Learn to sew and stitch
that heart of yours back together.

21 Days

My phone hasn't lit up from your notification all day.
But when it finally does it reads,
"I got some bad news. I won't be able to come see
 you tomorrow. There is no way for me to come."
My eyes get glossy at the sight of your text.

I haven't seen you for the past 13 days and counting.
Now I have to wait an additional 8 days,
only if the universe works out in our favor
and no other problems arise.

21 days without seeing you.
Everyday I long for your touch,
your kiss, your healing hug.

Tears stream down my face
as I am forced to accept you
being away from me for
even longer.

- Please let time go by faster

Fallen Petals

Like the roses you once gave me,
our love has an expected death time.
One by one, our petals float gracefully to the ground.
Over time our love has wilted away,
all of the passion and love has died.

I try to rewater those roses.
Attempting to regrow something
that no longer can thrive.
It brings me pain knowing these dead flowers have to go.
But I know it is necessary
so I can find new growth
and a new flower to water and care for.

- Don't water a dead plant

We Were Once In Love

Once upon a time,
I looked at you like you were my everything.
We fell in love in the most rawest and authentic way.
I used to look at you with passion and admiration in my eyes,
like you were my soulmate, my twin flame,
the one I'd be destined to marry.

But something changed in you.
You pushed me away so suddenly;
a total blindside.

Going from loving me to leaving me
in the matter of milliseconds.
I never understood why
or what made this love between us disappear.

I don't know about you,
but I have moved on to bigger and better things.
I couldn't spend my whole life waiting for you
when you pushed me away in the first place.
Though you loved me well, at the time,
I found someone else who loves me more
and will fight to keep me around.

- You've missed your chance.

The Fall

One More Night

Restlessness fuels my body as I toss and turn in my bed,
counting down the hours, down to the minutes.
The day I have been waiting for a long time
  is one sleep away.

Tomorrow when the sun rises,
I will wake up singing with the birds.
Jumping out of bed like a main character
in one of those cliché movies.

After patiently waiting for so long,
one more night,
then my dreams will finally become reality.

Burning

My skin burns for your touch.
For your tender kiss upon all my imperfections,
your gentle hands when our fingers tangle as one.
My heart burns for your presence.
For being able to gaze in your oceanic eyes once again.
Your voice echoes in my mind.
My heart burns for You.

Half My Soul

He is the one who wipes my sadness after I cried an ocean of tears.
The one who calls me beautiful, even when my hair is greasy
or kisses me when I haven't brushed my teeth yet.
Who motivates me to grow past my trauma,
encourages me to stay strong when life gets hard.
He is the one who makes me feel needed,
loved,
appreciated,
beautiful,
and everything in between.
He is everything.

He is half of my soul.

1:37A.M.

The world is hushed, yet my thoughts are buzzing.
Time means nothing when you're the only one awake.
Sleeping means nothing when I could lay awake
staring at my empty bedroom ceiling.
Hoping that maybe, just maybe
you are looking at yours,
thinking about me too.

Cold

Your side of the bed is cool to the touch.
Every night, you're not there,
"Goodnight Lover", I say aloud every night,
while I always reach to your side of the bed,
pretending to reach for you.

Hoping that one day, I'll feel your warmth.
I'll one day reach over and feel your body
next to mine.

Exactly where it should be.

Long Distance

It's a lie with relationships:
"Distance makes the heart grow fonder".

Distance makes the heart yearn for just a glimpse of them.
Distance makes you sob uglily at the door as you're saying your
    goodbyes.
Distance makes you count down the days, down to the hours, till
    they're back in your loving embrace.
Distance makes you wake up alone, every morning without them by your
    side.
Distance makes you wish that circumstances were different just so
    that you could see them every day.
Distance makes you cry knowing it'll be weeks before you can feel
    their lips pressed against yours.
Distance doesn't make the heart grow fonder.
Distance teaches patience.
Distance makes you question if the relationship is all worth it in the
    end.
But it makes you appreciate the small things:
a simple text or a phone call, or maybe a photo they sent of
    themselves.

Every day is another day closer to seeing them again.

His Eyes

Like waves crashing upon a sandy shore,
morpho butterfly wings fluttering effortlessly with the wind,
the sky on a warm summer's day,
delphiniums dancing in the gentle breeze,
a shimmering sapphire gem,
the color of the moon when you do something merely once,
robin's eggs as they sit peacefully high in the branches,
Neptune as it simply exists in our universe.

That is what his eyes remind me of.

First Kiss

Inches away from you, feeling each other's breath against one another.
Hesitating on who is going to make the first move.
Passion pushes you forward,
connecting as one, moving in unison.
Time stops as we are the most present we've ever been.
Fireworks explode and butterflies flutter within our stomachs.
Kissing you is when I knew you were mine.
Forever.

Disconnect

Come with me.
Disconnect from the world around us
as we emerge our souls together.
Lets run away from reality and go
where cell service or wifi is foreign.
Go with me to a land where the sun
rains down its warmth upon our skins.
Where silence fills our minds and ears.
Let's run away to a distant land
and disconnect from this planet we call home.

Three Years

Three years feels like three seconds
while getting to love you every single one of those days.

My Universe

I tell the universe all about you.
Gushing to the moon of all the things you do perfectly.
Convincing the stars that they are aligned for us.
Assuring the planets that there is no one like you.
Speaking to the universe that you are everything.
Ramble on about how nothing can kill our love,
not even the darkest black hole.

- You are my universe

Your Love

How flowers need rain,
how a poet needs paper,
I need you with me.

Lover

L is for the love of my life,
O is for him only building me up,
V is for a valuable relationship,
E is for our everlasting love,
R is for remembering how perfect he is for me.

Homesick

I am homesick.
Not for a place,
but a person.
Homesick for You.

For your comforting hug
that can mend all of my broken pieces.
For a passionate kiss
that makes me forget all what makes me cry.
For your words of affirmation,
telling me that everything will be okay.

But I can't get that right now.
I'm homesick for the comfort you bring me.

I am homesick for You.

The Sun & Moon

I am the sun.
Bright and vibrant.
Bringing warmth to those around me.
But I'll burn you if you get too close.
Stay away because I will harm you.

I am the moon.
Mysterious, as there is always a side of me hiding.
Bringing cool, comforting air to those around me.
But I'll show you pure beauty up close.
Come closer to me because I won't harm you.

Home

"When are you coming home?",
"I miss you",
"I want you home with me"
have become a part of my daily vocabulary.
Living apart from your partner is lonely.
As you patiently await for the day they walk
through your front doors again,
back in your embrace
so you feel at home again.

Difficult

The right relationship isn't easy.
It's not the endless affection,
it's not the comfort of having a lover and best friend all in one,
it's not the smothering in kisses,
it's not the daily affirmation of saying I love you.
That is what the media wants you to believe.

It's the uncomfortable conversations,
it's fighting for a love you can't stand watch die out,
it's arguing over all kinds of problems,
it's sobbing to your partner, trying to work through all problems.
That is what reality wants you to see.

It's embracing your differences
and realizing the best relationships
are the ones that you need to work the hardest in.

Here With You

Back in your embrace,
I feel safe.
I am where I am supposed to be.
Your protecting embrace engulfs me.
Listening to your heart beat
as I press my ear quietly against your chest,
presently here with you,
adoring every moment.

I Want You To Know

I may stay quiet,
but I scream to the universe that I love you.
That you are meant to love me perfectly.

Heartbeat

Lub dub, lub dub.
Goes your heartbeat
as I rest my ear on your chest,
quietly listening to the beautiful sound that keeps me alive.
That keeps you alive.
Lub dub, lub dub.
Goes my heartbeat
as we lay in silence
melting as one.

When I knew

You knew something was up.
That there was something racing in my mind
making me silent.
You memorize my favorite snack like the back of your hand.
So you offer it to me, saying I should light my favorite candle too.

Putting on a slow song,
and turning off the lights in the living room,
you extend your hand to me,
pulling me up to dance.

We slow danced in my living room in the candle light
as you softly sang in my ear.
Swaying back and forth gently.
Both absorbing this moment together as much as we could.

At that very moment, I knew.
I knew that you are meant to be my person.
To love me forever and spend the rest of our lives together.
You are my person.
You are the man that can make me smile,
even after I have cried endless tears.

Addiction

Like a chain smoker needs a lighter,
or an alcoholic needs a bottle.
You have become my finest addiction
and I can never get enough of you.

I Pray

I pray everyday that he heals from all
the things that he doesn't talk about.

Everything that he has had to go through
alone,
I hope he heals from it.

This man deserves everything under the sun,
from the kind of smile that hurts your cheeks
to a rare feeling of inner peace.

I need him to know how much I appreciate
all the little things he does for me.
And how much I have fallen in love with him.

The things I would do to make him know
how adored he is and how every single
morning, I wake up with a smile on my face
just by knowing that I get to love
him every single day.

I pray that he heals from all those painful sorrows.
Because I would be nowhere without him.

Stargazing

You and I lay side by side on a cool night.
Snuggled under a blanket as we watch the stars,
talking about life and what lays beyond the sky of lights.
It feels as if the universe is ours.

We exchange glances with each other,
time stops.
I crave that we intertwine with one another.
I lean in to kiss you and all my worry drops.

It's just you, me and the stars tonight.

I Found Love

I found love where it wasn't supposed to be.
In moments of hardships,
I found you.

Bliss

Away from the world,
here we stay.
Just you and I.
Not a living soul near us,
away from all negative energies.

Where peace and harmony coincide,
I have found this piece of bliss.

5.A.M

It is far too early for anyone to be buzzing with productivity.
Nearly all of the city is asleep
yet I stand here, more awake than I have ever been.

Thousands of lights illuminate the city
yet not a soul wanders the streets.
Silence that followed brought a sense of peace that I forgot to
    appreciate.
The sun begins to peek its nose over the horizon.
Curious if it is time for the city to come alive with motion and life.

I wonder what you would think about if you saw this view.
I'm sure you'd think it is beautiful too,
"Just like you", you would always tell me.

Sincerely, Yours

Little letters from you
written on all my sticky notes,
plastered all over my fridge.
All containing little doodles
or little words of affirmation.

Your handwriting is my favorite:

"I love you. Sincerely, yours".

Touch In The Dark

Do me a favor.
Sit or lay together in a dark room with your partner;
with slim to no clothes on.

Simply feel each other.
I'm not talking in a sexual way.
I'm talking about a gentle and seeking kind of way.

Let your hands explore each other's bodies.
Feel all of their curves, cuts, scars, and the bone structure of each other.
Take your time as there is no need to rush.
Just be present with them.

Let your hands glaze their collarbone as they feel the curve of your hips.
Softly touch their lips that you've kissed a million times
as they trace their fingertips down your arms.

Appreciate the way they have grown to be.
Embracing all of their flaws
and falling in love with every curve and edge of them.

- You'll feel a deeper connection if you simply explore

Life Giver

Love begins as a simple emotion.
The kind that gives you butterflies
or a firework show during your first kiss.
Before you know it,
love becomes the air you breathe.
It becomes the one thing that gives you life.

Love becomes the one thing that keeps you alive.
It makes you find your true purpose.

- Love is my oxygen

Eyes

Show me your amiable eyes
as they are the gateway to your soul.
Be vulnerable with me.
Open yourself to me like a book.
Allow me to read every page
and let me look at you
so I can admire every beautiful part you possess.

Yellow

The color of a thousand warm suns,
of bright sunflowers in an endless field,
a tangy lemon hanging on the edge of a glass of lemonade,
of your favorite flavor of Starbursts,
different hues of fire dancing on a burning log,
a glimmering sunset shining brightly at golden hour.

- You are my yellow

Reminisce

I remember the first time that you and I talked.
You brought out the pure happiness
that I never believed I would get back.
I smiled more the closer we got.
The reason why I have motivation to better myself
and grow as an individual.
You quickly became my everything.
In the end, you turned into nothing.
I lost you and the universe took you away from me.

- And I'll never get you back

Protector

You are my protector.
Of my heart,
of my soul,
of myself.

Slow Dancing

In the living room of our new home.
After years of living under separate roofs,
we finally get to live under the same roof.
As we unpack, a slow and romantic song
echoes in the empty living room.
I feel your hand softly caress mine.
Intertwining our fingers, you pull me to dance.

Our first memory together in our new home
is us dancing in the empty living room,
boxes cluttering the other half of our space.

Here I slow dance with you
in a place that we both can now call home.

Grip

You have a certain grip on me
that I can't explain fully.

Naked

Being the most vulnerable with you
was not when we took off our clothes.
It was allowing you to examine my darkest truths.
Letting you see all the parts of me that
hide behind closed doors.
Yet after shedding all of my layers,
you still love me the same
and don't judge me any less.

Touch In The Spark

We lock eye contact and you scoot closer to me.
Time stops.
Feeling your body heat against my sides,
I don't move away.
Maintaining the closeness,
I feel the electricity between the two of us.
Leaning in slowly, your lips become inches from mine.
I don't move away.
Urges try to push me forward but I refrain.
Subtly, I move in slightly.
Meeting me halfway,
our lips brush each other's for the first time
and suddenly,
I feel at home.

Vivid

Imagine being so in love with someone
that the first time you two kissed
you kept smiling in and out of the kiss
like a complete dork.
Being so stupidly happy that this moment,
that you have dreamt of for so long,
has finally become reality.

The world coming to a halt
as the electricity sparks between you two.
Everything all feeling and playing out
just like a movie.

- I had that with You.

Invisible Kiss

You and I have built this special kind of connection.
Where the relationship isn't built off of only sex.
Having quality time and connection overruling most things,
building a deeper connection everyday
and listening wholeheartedly to everything each has to say.

A connection we've found is something not many get to have.
Hookup culture ruins all notion of most healthy
or genuine relationships.

I don't need to kiss your lips all the time to know that I love you.
Or to know if you love me too.
This connection is filled with invisible kisses.
Where you may not see them often
but you know they are always there.

Sparks In The Boy

The boy unfolds himself slowly to his mistress,
progressively showing her all of his true colors.
These sparks for her make him break down all of his walls.
Brick by brick, the wall comes down to nothing.
He chooses to go out of his way to make her happy
or get her something that reminded him of her.
Those sparks make him look at her so passionately.
Nothing like anyone has ever looked at her before.
Falling weak in his knees for her touch,
craving to know all that makes her who she is.
The boy embraces those flickers and allows them to ignite
into something much greater than a spark.

- Falling in love is not something words can usually describe

The Angel & The Star

He was a star.
Shining brightly amongst a million others.
But to her, he shined brighter than the rest.
A one in a million star that caught
the angel's attention.

She was an angel.
The kind that graces the land with her presence.
She'd stare at her star,
hoping that he would see how brightly he shines
whenever she is around.

Together, they created a safe haven
only built for each other.

Pull Me Closer

Don't let me go.
I feel sheltered here in your arms.
Safe from all harm's way.
If you push me away
or let go,
you'll take a piece of my heart with you.
Something I can never get back.

Freckles

Her freckles splatter across her cheeks,
connecting by the bridge of her nose.
More found all over her face,
more subtle than the rest.

Her freckles was always his favorite part of her
because the summer sun made them that much more vibrant.
If he could, he would kiss every single freckle on her face and body,
telling her how artistic this natural beauty makes her.

The Change

You

You deserve the same kind of love that you give to everyone you meet.
It will come, I promise.

Trust

Trust that the universe has everything planned for you.
Everything happens for a reason.
Your time will come.

Grounding

Do you hear that?
Silence?
Maybe you're surrounded by noise.
Tell me about it.

What do you see?
A living room?
Maybe you're outside enjoying the fresh air.
Tell me about it.

What do you feel?
The way this book fits perfectly in your hands?
Maybe it is the fuzzy blanket that protects your body from the cold air.
Tell me about it.

What do you taste?
The stale gum you've been chewing for hours?
Maybe it is the cheese and crackers you've been munching on while reading.
Tell me about it.

What do you smell?
The fruity scent of your favorite candle burning nearby?
Maybe it is your food, cooking in the oven.
Tell me about it.

– Live presently (or even just try)

Don't Go

There is one in one hundred and seven chances of you getting into a
  car crash.
A one in fourteen million chance of winning the lottery.
A one in almost four million chance of getting attacked by a shark.
A one in five hundred thousand chance of getting struck by lighting.
A one in a million chance of going viral on the internet.
A one in eleven million chance of dying in a plane crash.
But
there is a one in four hundred trillion chance of you being here.
Being born into this universe.
The odds are for you, not against you.
You are meant to be here.

The Test

World continuously tests me.
Quizzing me on what is the best thing I should do.
I give a confident answer,
but it's always wrong.
And I get punished
by things I don't want.
Each day is a lesson;
a learning curve.

I need to not take those failures to heart.
Taking each failure and planting it as a seed.
Patiently waiting for growth to emerge.
One day I will answer the worlds test
and I will get it right.
I will learn my lesson
so I can grow and succeed.

Highway of Life

We are all on our own roads.
Driving our own cars at our own pace.
Some accelerate in life faster than others,
passing everyone at mach speed.
Some take the scenic route, enjoying taking it slow.
We all drive different cars;
some old, some new.

We are all on our own roads.
Sometimes our roads converge with others.
Some permanent, some temporary.
Sometimes the roads diverge away from one another.
There may be accidents along the way.
Might be detrimental,
maybe it will be minor.

Despite all the speed bumps, accidents or road closures,
we must continue our journey.
Remembering we must stop and fuel up to feel full again.
But we must go on.
Not comparing our cars or progress.

Over all, we must remember that it is not about the destination
but the journey as we all drive through the Highway of Life.

Read It Again

You compare yourself to the other seven billion people in this world.
Only seeing the negatives, shying from the positives.
Undergoing daily changes, just to adhere to society's needs.

Always striving to be someone else.
Realizing that maybe you'll be happier hiding under a mask.
Eventually you will see it is not worth it.

In present day society,
many people don't feel worthless.
Putting themselves down by comparing to unrealistic expectations.
Only this time, you must realize that
reality is fucked up, not you.
Time means nothing when it comes to embracing one's growth.
All of us grow at different paces.
Never compare yourself to others.
Together let us scream to society that we are all beautiful, despite
    our flaws.

– Now read the first letter of each line

101

Society

Society is broken
I refuse to believe that
There is good in anyone
When you look closely
This world is an evil place
Even if
Goodness does shine through
When I have kids, I will tell them
Being a bad person
Is more important than
Being a good person in society
But I will tell them that:
Violence is inevitable
There is no good in people
People tell me
I should lose faith in humanity
I do not conclude that
Good people exist
In the future,
Society will not mend itself
It can no longer be said that
People in this world are caring
It will be evident that
People choose violence over love
It is foolish to assume that
Society is not broken.

All of this will come true, unless we reserve it.

Me, Myself & I

I have been here for myself since the day I came into this world.
Through all the heartbreaks, hardtimes, and tears
I have been there for myself all those times.
No one has stuck around for all the good or bad
and I don't credit myself for going through all my horrid thoughts
or my joyful days all alone.
Just me, myself & I.

Vanished Childhood

We are no longer kids.
According to the government, we are adults.
All expected to grow up.
Get a boring full time job for fifty years to only assist the economy.
Expected to have a house, marriage and kids by the age of twenty-five.
Live the same routine life until we retire or are too old for great
   adventures.

We are expected to abandon the fun of our childhoods,
forced to accept adult responsibilities.

No more summers at the park playing imaginary games with friends,
no more worries from simple math homework,
no more finding joys in the small things in life.
We are adults now.
Society tells us that adults aren't allowed to have fun as if we're kids.

And it's all unfair.

Dead

Old me is dead.
Through growth, heartbreak and trauma,
I am not the same person I was one year ago.
Three years ago.
Five years ago.
Ten years ago.

People grow and evolve
every single day.
Do not compare me to my past
because I am someone much more than that.
The old me is dead,
so don't you dare try to think that we are the same person.

Forgive & Don't Forget

```
I have caused harm to myself,
but I forgave the ones who made me do it.
```

Madness

This is what this world has come to:
where gun violence cause 20,000 deaths
and every year that number climbs.
Where common sense is not that common.
Where tropical storms continuously break records,
obliterating everything that gets in its way.
Where laws made by old men rule young women's bodies,
and living in a society where women are not seen as humans.
Where climate change affects our planet we call home,
but everyone continues to be careless.

It all makes me sick.
Because this is what this world has come to.

Hometown

This little town lies to you.
With making the citizens its prisoners,
allowing for little progress or growth.
Forcing you to live in comfort.
As terrifying as it may seem,
you must leave this tiny town
to be able to spread your wings.

- Growth happens outside your comfort zone

Mirror

I am beautiful.
I am powerful.
I am strong.

I repeat to myself,
my flawed body staring back at me.

This mirror holds the capability
between me, self-love, and acceptance.

Bitter or Better

All of my life
I always told myself that I would not hold grudges.
But here I am, thinking bitterly of you.

You were absent,
you were not there for me when I needed you,
you were not who I thought you would have been.

And I struggle to get myself past that.

But I forget the word,
"Were".
Were is past tense.
I was once told by someone dear to me,
"You either get bitter or get better".

I am choosing to get better.
Let go of the past
and focus on the future and
what is happening right now.

I'm choosing to get better, and not stay bitter.

My Personal Quest

In this lifetime, you must heal.
Acknowledge that the past is already in cement.
Focus everyday on forgiving yourself,
even on the hard days.
I want you to grow and improve,
even if you only better yourself a bit.
A little bit every day will add up quite quickly.

- Heal for your inner child

Hands Of A Warrior

If you look at the hands that write this,
there are scars and flaws.
But there is strength that graces these fingers.

Behind this book, there is a person.
A living being who has experienced hell,
just like I have.
Who has cried themselves to sleep,
hoping no one would hear their sobs.

A warrior graces this earth.
And I am not talking about only
the person who writes this.

- Strength comes to those who endure hell

Fresh Start

Like opening to a new chapter.
Maybe an entirely new book,
moving to a new city,
or ending a long term relationship.

The concept of the unknown is terrifying
because these starts often happen suddenly.
A fresh start can be rejuvenating.

We all get comfort in being stuck in routine.
Don't be afraid to break that.
Get a fresh start
because it isn't as terrifying
as you might imagine it to be.

5, 4, 3, 2, 1.

Five seconds until you need to give yourself this outrageous bravery.
Four seconds is all it takes for you to change your own life.
Three seconds to drop all of your doubt and worries.
Two seconds to prepare your mind and body;
You only have one second left.

- Whatever it is. Now is your time.

Listen

You must listen to the actions of somebody
rather than their words.
What they do will display where their priorities lie.

Adore You

```
Stop being so insecure in your body.
You are capable of so many amazing things.
The poets would adore someone like you.
```

Silent Lovers

Believe me or not,
but everyone reading this has silent lovers in their lives.
From children who may look up to you,
a teen who may wish they had your body,
the quiet classmate who adores your laugh from afar,
or an adult seeing that you are living the life they once desired.

You are silently loved by so many.
People are just too scared to speak out
and admit they admire you from a distance.

- Remember this the next time you feel alone in this world

Continue On

You will never miss out on what is meant for you.
Don't feel like you are missing out.
If you are meant to be with someone,
the universe will ensure you two are together.
They will come back
or maybe they won't.

But that is all a part of the universe's plan.
So continue to live your life and don't worry.
Let the universe take care of the rest
and take care of you.

365 Days

If you pursue one single thing for one full year,
you can accomplish anything you set your mind to.
Strive and acknowledge that every second
is extremely valuable.
You will become best friends with the idea of time.
Time allows daily chances to rewrite your history.
A new dawn is a new chance
to build the life you want.
Strive to do your best at everything you do.
Put all that drive into one thing for one year
and see what happens.

-   Time is passing every second of every day

Believe It Or Not

Distance is the answer.
This scary eight lettered word can either
bring you two together
and show each of you how much you need each other,
or it will show you that
maybe you two were never meant to be.

This might be scary.
That is okay.
Please don't be scared
because distance might be the answer to your question.

I Am A Woman

"It's not all men", they say in their defense.
But it is a majority of women
who have been beaten or belittled.
Women have always been objectified or sexualized,
as something not real and feeble.

Men don't worry about being followed
as you're walking home alone
or being groped at a nightclub
and forced into uncomfortable or violent situations.

"She is asking for it by what she wears"
he will tell her.
Wrong.
Educate your sons, and don't belittle us women.

I am a woman and we are the same just as any man.

- We are human too

Invision It

Take a moment and think:
What kind of a life do you want?
Short term and long term.

Do you want a significant other?
Want to marry your partner?
Want kids? Or maybe a house full of pets?
Own your own business?
The best body you've had in years?

Your mind is a powerful thing
and that often gets discredited.
Recognize that your mind can help you get what you want.
Invision everything that will make your soul happy.

- If you can see it in your head, you can hold it in your hands

Happy New Year

A new year lurks upon us,
just like every other year.
But this time it will be different.

All of the bad things that happened this year,
leave it at the door.
Before you walk into the new door of a new year,
leave all of the bad experiences behind.

Allow a full body healing and greet the new reflection
that will greet you in the new year.

Look Up

Being nose deep in an electronic screen.
Nobody looks up anymore.
Society would much rather stare down and see the latest trends
rather than look up and see what is in front of us.
How many concert videos do you see that are flooded
with cameras all recording the same thing?
Or how many times have you seen a couple in a restaurant
staring down at their phones instead of across the table?

Wherever you are in the world,
look up for a second.
Look around or maybe look at one certain object.
At every point in your life
you must realize that you are the only person in the world
seeing what you are seeing from this angle.
Whether it be your living room, bedroom, or the great outdoors.
No one is looking at that thing at the angle in the way that you are.
So please, put down your phones and look up.

- Live away from technology

Healthy After Toxic

It can be assumed that a healthy relationship after a toxic one
is an easy adjustment to put yourself through.
You are wrong.

It is learning that trust is beyond important.
That losing them over stupid arguements aren't an issue.
That they won't degrade you for talking
about what runs through your mind.
Those hard conversations won't push them away.

Just because past relationships harmed you,
doesn't mean they will.

-   It is a learning curve of growth

Who Were They?

Everyone you walk or drive past
has a lifelong story you know nothing about.
A full life filled with all kinds of experiences.

You don't know their name,
nor do they know yours.
But every stranger you see lives a life
you know nothing about.

-   Be kind, always.

The Healing

Untouchable

Every night I stare up at the moon.
Crave for what it would be like to reach for it;
Refusing the laws of gravity.
Simply existing in a far away land.

I ponder who else in the world is also staring at the moon with me.
Wondering what lies beyond earth's gravity.
Asking how they can escape this planet to explore the unknown.

Even if I wanted to, the moon is untouchable.

Rain

Gentle rain patters on the roof.
A grumble of thunder from far away.
The smell of rain;
the calm before the storm.

The Forest

Towering trees sway overhead.
The cool air blankets my face.
Damp grass moistens my shoes.
The forest is quiet.
Eerie.
Without you by my side,
I don't feel safe here.

Perennial

I am a perennial flower.
Despite all the harsh elements,
I return year after year.
Blooming as beautiful as ever.

This Is It

This is the feeling I have been waiting for my whole life.
The feeling of freedom, rushing to me like a breath of fresh air.

To Those Who Fall In Love With the Mentally Ill

We are broken.
We are not perfect,
nowhere close.
We will question whether we are good enough.
We will go through mental breakdowns and panic attacks
almost daily.

If you have the privilege of falling in love with us,
be patient,
be genuine,
be kind.
We have our bad days that may turn into weeks,
possibly months.
But we are trying to fight the demons that tell us horrid things.
Telling us that we aren't good enough
or that we are better off six feet under
rather than gracing the world with our presence.

All we ask is for a hand to hold
and a welcoming embrace on those bad days.

And please,
I beg for you
to not leave
after we have gained a
deep and sentimental trust with you.
And after we have fallen in love with you.

Because if our support system is gone,
we are back to square one.

Changes

Life keeps me on my toes.
Throwing curveballs and rapid changes my way,
anticipating that I can keep up.

I try.
I really do.
By accomplishing every changing moment.
Trying not to drown.

Asleep

I close my eyes.
Feeling my chest rise and fall
at a slow and steady pace.
My mind falls quiet.
Peace fills my mind as I attempt to sleep,
floating to a dark abyss.

Ashes

My home is unrecognizable,
as if a bomb went off.
Roof has collapsed onto the floor.
Burnt insulation covers the water soaked floor.
All furniture is in disarray, picture frames hang by a thread.
The smell of burnt everything and leftover smoke sting my nose.
As I cautiously meander through the house,
observing all the damage this uncontrollable fire did.

Everything looks familiar,
but it's unrecognizable at the same time.

I wish I could turn back time.
So I can take a longer look at my home before I walked away.
Because back then, I did not know it would be my last time
seeing it as my normal childhood home.

Stacked

My history surrounds me,
inked permanently in all these journals.
Rereading everything I wrote about.
Diary entries filled with emotion and rawness.

Over the countless books I've filled,
I see my growth.
It is hard to reread my past.
But I know that I must heal
all those past wounds.

I have not lived a beautiful or flawless life.
But every moment stacks on one another.

When Day Becomes Night

Colors of orange, red and yellow fade into purples and blues.
Painting the sky like a watercolor artwork
before the darkness takes over.

The sky shows you flawless beauty nearly every evening.
Showing the world that not all endings can be horrible.
Endings can be beautiful too.

Art of Dying

We are born.
As babies, we learn how to walk and fulfill our basic needs.
As toddlers, we attend school.
Attempting to be more vocal and mobile.
During our years at high school,
we learn all kinds of pointless things that we'll never use in our
  adulthood.
In our teens, we become more rebellious.
Having our first kiss and enjoying the thrill of sneaking out.
Feeling the addiction of adrenaline
pumping through our veins.
As young adults, we graduate high school and university.
Working a fulltime job to pay all our bills.
As adults, we still work that fulltime job.
Get married to the love of your life.
Enjoying children, if that is what you so desire.
Traveling and exploring the world, if you're lucky.
Then as elders, we reflect on our once blissful life,
sharing our adventures and stories
to our own children or the younger generations.
Trying to enjoy the last moments of our life
before we die.

- Life is Art

Wake Me Up

Stuck reliving a bad dream.
Not the kind of bad dream you can wake up from.
It is the kind of dream that haunts you in your waking life.
Can you wake me up?
Get me out of here.
I thought dreams were supposed to be pleasant.
Blissful even.
Can you wake me up?
I am caught in this bad dream
and I can not get out.

Grow Up

One day, child, you are going to grow up
and see how the world really is.

It is not always blue skies and sunshine.
There will be dark clouds,
thunderstorms, and hurricanes.
But after each storm,
you will see the rainbow.

- You just have to look for it

Snowy Evening

I remind myself of a blizzard:
cold to the touch,
silent,
and
oddly beautiful to watch.
But I can cause chaos to people when they least expect it.

11:11

Glancing at the clock, I see those magical numbers.
Acknowledging that some divine being is encouraging me to look at the
    time.
It is a sign.
I used to never think anything of it.

For years, I see these numbers numerous times a day.
Each set of numbers has a meaning.
Pay attention to the signs the universe is giving you.

They are always giving you signs,
you just might not be paying enough attention.

- Once it starts, it doesn't stop

Monday

Everyone discredits Mondays
for apparently being the worst day in the week.
I deem that not to be true.

A lovely couple got married on a Monday.
A stressed student aced their exam on a Monday.
That young teen had their first kiss with their crush on a Monday.
Someone with a hard home life gets to go to work
to distract them from all life problems every Monday.

People think Mondays are the worst.
But sometimes, Mondays can actually be the best day of the week.

Friday

Everyone puts Fridays as the best day of the week.
Friday seems to be the best day of the week.
That can't be true all of the time.

Someone lost a lifelong partner on a Friday.
A passionate employee got fired unfairly on a Friday.
A student failed an exam on Friday.
That quiet friend is going home on Friday to their abusive family for
    the weekend.

People assume Fridays are the best.
But sometimes, Fridays can actually be the worst day of the week.

Saturn

Deemed to be the most beautiful planet due to her rocky rings.
Her rings separating her from all her other sister planets;
Uniquely perfect.
The whole universe is drawn to how she simply exists in our solar system.

Mother

Love greater than the pacific ocean.
You will always fight for me.
Fight all demons for me.
Striving to put me on the highest pedestal.

Mother's are someone special.
A woman who teaches their children to swim
despite the crazy currents of the world.

I see you in every reflection;
a powerful woman who made me who I am today.

- I love you, Mom

Headache

Head pounding against itself,
telling me I need to take a step back;
Focus on healing and settling that racing brain of mine.

Monster In The Dark

Children say they're terrified
of the monster that lurks
under their bed.

But as they grow up,
they no longer become scared.
Not of the monster
or even the dark.

The children become
comforted by knowing
they have grown up
to be those monsters
in the dark.

Getting Older

The scary thing about growing up
isn't realizing that you are going to have to be an adult one day.
Not that you'll be paying your own bills or doing your own taxes.
It's realizing that as your parents watch you grow up,
they're not getting any younger either.

- They age just like you do

After Dusk

Where the sun takes cover under the horizon,
hiding away from the moon and all his powerful glory.
Hints of yellow and orange emit from the skyline,
bidding its last farewell till the sun rises the next morning.

Piano

A piano is a work of art that encourages
the connection between humans and their souls.
Invited to tell its tale without words.
by listening to many blissful keys played
in perfect order, each at the perfect time.

The music produced is like no other.
Bringing peace and serenity
and pure euphoria to those who listen closely.

Keep Me Sane

The escape route from the world is carved by the poet's pen,
sculpting passion and emotion with each stroke.
Through the outlet of poetry,
poets choose vulnerability through words.
To write releases all of those pent up emotions.
Putting them all on this piece of paper
to get it into the world
and out of the mind.

The pen and papers have been there for me when many people haven't.
The ink lets me bleed the sorrow and hurt with no judgment.
Without writing, I would feel much more alone than I truly am.

Writing is the one thing that helps to keep me sane.

Index of Titles

About the Author

Sarah Cowan was born and raised in Alberta, a stunning province in Canada with rugged mountains. Her interest for creating stories and poetry flourished as she was growing up and she could frequently be spotted writing her next work. She realized as she grew older that she wanted to make a career by sharing her works with the world. Sarah studied at Concordia University of Edmonton and earned a Bachelor of Arts degree with a major in English. Then utilized her degree to pursue writing, and she will certainly continue to do so for many years to come.

www.ingramcontent.com/pod-product-compliance
Lightning Source LLC
La Vergne TN
LVHW051347080426
835509LV00020BA/3328